National Parks
Rocky Mountain

JENNIFER ZEIGER

Children's Press®
An Imprint of Scholastic Inc.

Content Consultant

James Gramann, PhD

Professor, Department of Recreation, Park and Tourism Sciences,

Texas A&M University, College Station, Texas

Library of Congress Cataloging-in-Publication Data

Names: Zeiger, Jennifer, author.

Title: Rocky Mountain / by Jennifer Zeiger.

Description: New York : Children's Press, an imprint of Scholastic Inc., 2018. | Series: A true book |
    Includes bibliographical references and index.

Identifiers: LCCN 2016050888 | ISBN 9780531233948 (library binding) | ISBN 9780531240212 (pbk.)

Subjects: LCSH: Rocky Mountain National Park (Colo.)—Juvenile literature.

Classification: LCC F782.R59 Z45 2018 | DDC 978.8/69—dc23

LC record available at https://lccn.loc.gov/2016050888

Front cover (main): Big Thompson River

Front cover (inset): A climber

Back cover: A moose

Find the Truth!

Everything you are about to read is true *except* for one of the sentences on this page.

Which one is **TRUE**?

T or F Rocky Mountain National Park has trees that have branches on only one side.

T or F The park is home to a large population of gray wolves.

Find the answers in this book.

Contents

THE BIG TRUTH!

National Parks Field Guide: Rocky Mountain

Bighorn sheep

4

The lights of nearby Estes Park at night.

Rock climber

5

Mountain climbing is thrilling—and dangerous! Only a very experienced climber would attempt a climb like this.

Rocky Mountain National Park is one of the highest parks in the United States.

Rocky Mountain Majesty

The long, jagged spine of the Rocky Mountains stretches from Alaska all the way to New Mexico. Nestled within this range, in northern Colorado, lies Rocky Mountain National Park. At 415 square miles (1,075 square kilometers), it is far from the United States' largest protected area. However, it is one of the most visited. It is packed with rivers, lakes, wildlife, hiking trails, and breathtaking views. It's easy to see why "Rocky," as the park is known, is so popular.

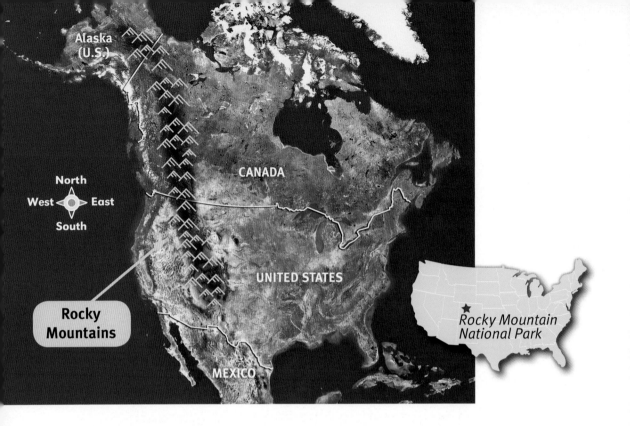

Rocky Mountains

Rocky Mountain National Park

Molding the Mountains

The Rockies are not one continuous mountain range. They are actually a series of many smaller ranges that run together. Rocky Mountain National Park is part of the Front Range. This range extends from southern Wyoming south into Colorado. This stretch of mountains has been developing for roughly two billion years.

That's how long ago changes began to happen within Earth's crust, which is made up of large pieces called tectonic plates. In what is now the western United States, the edge of one plate has been slowly moving under the edge of another all this time. This forces the land above it up into mountains.

As forces beneath Earth's surface push upward, wind and water fight back. At least two mountain ranges rose in the West before today's Rockies. **Erosion** shrank these mountains into low hills and valleys.

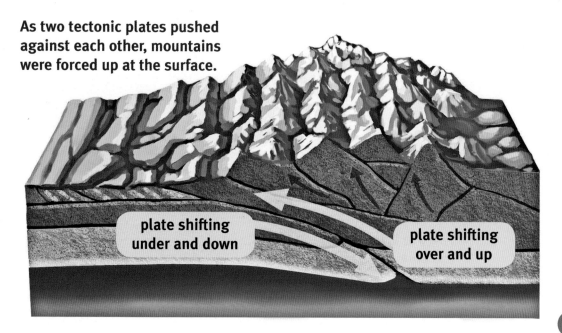

As two tectonic plates pushed against each other, mountains were forced up at the surface.

plate shifting under and down

plate shifting over and up

The range we see today first formed about 70 million years ago. Some of its mountains are more than 14,000 feet (4,267 meters) high. Erosion has left its mark here, too. Even some of the highest **elevations** have been smoothed into gentle slopes. Frozen glaciers have moved steadily down the mountains. As they traveled, they carved streams, rivers, lakes, and other shapes into the land.

A Timeline of Rocky Mountain National Park

About 8000 BCE

The first humans arrive in the area.

1200 to 1300 CE

The Ute arrive in the area.

1803

The United States purchases the Louisiana Territory, which included the Rocky Mountains, from France.

The park has both steep climbs and gently sloping trails. High up are low plants and open sky. Farther down lie dense forests and wide meadows. And down the middle lies the Continental Divide, which runs along the Rockies. On one side of this imaginary line dividing North America, all rivers flow west to the Pacific Ocean. On the other, rivers flow east toward the Atlantic Ocean.

1907

Enos Mills and other leaders begin efforts to convince the U.S. government to create a national park in the area.

1820

Stephen H. Long leads a group of explorers who become the first European-Americans to explore the region.

1915

Rocky Mountain National Park officially opens.

People Passing Through

The first humans in the southern Rockies arrived about 11,000 years ago. They mainly passed through while hunting or traveling. The Ute and other native groups settled the area beginning in about 1200 CE.

Change came to the region when the United States purchased it as part of the Louisiana Territory from France in 1803. The territory covered much of the American West. White Americans soon settled in and around the Front Range, clearing land for farming, mining, and logging. They also hunted increasing numbers of animals. By the 1900s, residents such as Enos Mills were worried about the environment. In 1907, he and others began working to protect the area. In 1915, they succeeded, and the U.S. Congress created Rocky Mountain National Park.

National Park Fact File

A national park is land that is protected by the federal government. It is a place of importance to the United States because of its beauty, history, or value to scientists. The U.S. Congress creates a national park by passing a law. Here are some key facts about Rocky Mountain National Park.

Rocky Mountain National Park	
Location	Northern Colorado
Year established	1915
Size	415 square miles (1,075 sq km)
Average number of visitors each year	3.1 million
Famous features	Dramatic mountain peaks, forests, alpine lakes, the Continental Divide, and the source of the Colorado River
Tallest mountain	Longs Peak, at 14,259 feet (4,346 m)

A climber in the Rocky Mountains

Hikers visit
Emerald Lake.

CHAPTER 2

The View From Above

There are countless reasons visitors come to Rocky Mountain National Park. One obvious attraction is the dizzying heights of the mountains and their spectacular views. But that's not all the park has to offer. Sparkling lakes, swift rivers, winding canyons, and gentle meadows are scattered throughout the area. Crisscrossing these sights are about 350 miles (563 km) of trails. A visitor could spend months exploring the park and still not see all of it.

Rocky Mountain National Park is home to 147 lakes.

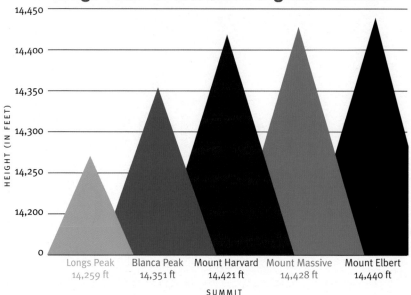

Longs Peak vs. Colorado's Highest Summits

HEIGHT (IN FEET)

| Longs Peak | Blanca Peak | Mount Harvard | Mount Massive | Mount Elbert |
| 14,259 ft | 14,351 ft | 14,421 ft | 14,428 ft | 14,440 ft |

SUMMIT

On Top of the World

Longs Peak is the park's tallest mountain. Some hikers climb Longs Peak not only for its spectacular views, but also as part of a larger challenge: to scale all 53 "fourteeners" in Colorado. A fourteener is a mountain that rises higher than 14,000 feet (4,267 m). Though Longs is the only fourteener in the park, it's not the only giant. Hikers also frequently take on Ypsilon Mountain and its neighbors, Chapin and Chiquita.

Tracking the Source

If you head to the western side of the park, you can find the source of the Colorado River. Explorers can start at the Colorado River Trailhead off Trail Ridge Road. Follow the trail just over 7 miles (11.3 km) to La Poudre Pass. There lies a swampy area that feeds a small stream—the Colorado River. The river may have humble beginnings, but it certainly leaves its mark.

The flowing waters of the Colorado River have carved out such natural wonders as the Grand Canyon.

Staying Safe

Whether hiking, biking, or camping, humans can get into trouble in the mountains. Some trails are steep, uneven, or otherwise challenging. At high elevations, there is less oxygen, making it difficult to breathe. Weather changes quickly in the mountains, too. Temperatures can plummet, and precipitation and wind can make it difficult for climbers to see or to keep their footing. Some people are inexperienced or unprepared for the challenges of this environment.

Climbers should use proper gear such as ropes, helmets, and harnesses to stay safe.

No matter how you're traveling through the park, always follow the rules and stay prepared for the unexpected.

Adventurers may become lost or injured, suffer **hypothermia**, or become sick from the high elevations. The park has rules and recommendations to help keep people safe. For example, never go close to a wild animal. Cars, bikes, and other vehicles must stay on roads. Always carry a map, compass, and extra water, food, and clothing. Emergency supplies such as a flashlight and a first aid kit are a good idea, too. And never go into closed areas.

Coppers are among the many types of butterflies found in Rocky.

CHAPTER 3

Wildlife in the Rockies

The landscape of Rocky Mountain National Park has a lot to offer. So do the many creatures that live there. Some visitors come just to spot the wildlife. The animals in the park range from mighty moose and sharp-eyed eagles to tiny chipmunks and delicate butterflies. Some **species** only pass through the park at certain times of year. Others live there year-round. However, no matter when you visit the park, there are plenty of interesting animals to see.

An elk bugles, searching for a mate.

Furry Creatures

The park's 800 or so elk are perhaps its most famous mammal residents. In the fall, visitors can hear these animals bugling, or calling for mates. Moose graze near streams and lakes on the western side of the park. In rivers, otters swim and beavers build dams. Smaller animals, such as chipmunks and weasels, scurry through the forests. Black bears, mountain lions, and coyotes hunt. At dusk, you might spot a bat swooping silently in the sky.

The Rockies Without Wolves

In the 19th and 20th centuries, Americans hunted gray wolves nearly to extinction. People wanted to protect their livestock and themselves from these predators. However, gray wolves hunted elk and kept their populations in check. Without wolves, elk numbers exploded. They ate more grass, limiting food for other animals. Today, rangers and qualified volunteers kill a controlled number of elk in the park. Some people argue that wolves should be reintroduced instead. However, officials believe that Rocky is too small, with too many people living nearby. This could lead to wolf-human conflicts.

Flying Creatures

Bird-watchers can keep busy in Rocky! Grebes, geese, sandpipers, snipes, and other **migrating** birds pass through. Jays, woodpeckers, nutcrackers, and many other birds live there all year. Large predatory birds such as golden eagles and turkey vultures soar high, looking for their next meal. Visitors can also spot wild turkeys strolling through the park.

Birds share the skies with a dizzying range of insects. More than 140 types of butterflies are found in the park!

A golden eagle keeps an eye out for prey below its high perch.

The boreal toad is most often found in **montane** areas of the park.

Cold-Blooded Creatures

The park boasts about 60 species of mammals, more than 270 types of birds, and countless insects. Reptiles and amphibians, however, are not so diverse. Temperatures are often too low for these cold-blooded animals. Only four species of amphibians live in the park. All of them have worryingly low populations. One, the boreal toad, is officially **endangered** in the area. The park claims only two reptile species: the garter snake and the eastern fence lizard.

National Parks Field Guide:
Rocky Mountain

Here are a few of the hundreds of fascinating animals you may see in the park.

Bighorn Sheep

Scientific name: *Ovis Canadensis*

Habitat: High up on the mountains in fall and winter; at lower elevations such as Horseshoe Park in spring and summer

Diet: Grasses, shrubs

Fact: These sheep's feet are specially adapted to help the animals leap and climb along steep cliff faces.

Moose

Scientific name: *Alces alces*

Habitat: Most common in areas with a lot of water plants and willows

Diet: Leaves, stems, buds, and bark from trees, shrubs, and water plants

Fact: A male's antlers can span as much as 6 feet (1.8 m) across.

White-tailed Ptarmigan

Scientific name: *Lagopus leucura*

Habitat: High elevations, above the tree line

Diet: Buds, leaves, seeds, fruits, flowers, and insects

Fact: These birds are white in winter. In summer, they are brown and gray.

Clark's Nutcracker

Scientific name: *Nucifraga columbiana*

Habitat: Throughout evergreen forests

Diet: Seeds, nuts, berries, insects, eggs, and sometimes young birds

Fact: Nutcrackers bury up to 33,000 seeds each fall in various spots called caches. During the winter, they can find nearly all the seeds they hid.

Goldenrod Crab Spider

Scientific name: *Misumena vatia*

Habitat: Areas with wildflowers and shrubs

Diet: Flies, bees, wasps, butterflies

Fact: These spiders don't use webs to catch food. Instead, they wait on a flower for prey to happen by. Then they pounce!

Western Terrestrial Garter Snake

Scientific name: *Thamnophis elegans*

Habitat: Lower elevations within the park

Diet: Small animals such as slugs, frogs, fish, and mice

Fact: These snakes spend the winter hibernating in dens with many other garter snakes.

From Forest to Tundra

Rocky Mountain National Park's rugged range of elevations does not just create beautiful views. It also creates a set of very different **ecosystems**. The park's lowest elevations enjoy a temperate **climate**. However, the environment changes in higher areas. Temperatures drop, and winds become more powerful. Across these regions, visitors can find a huge range of plant life. Each species is specially suited to its home.

Mature ponderosa pines can survive high winds, drought, and even fire.

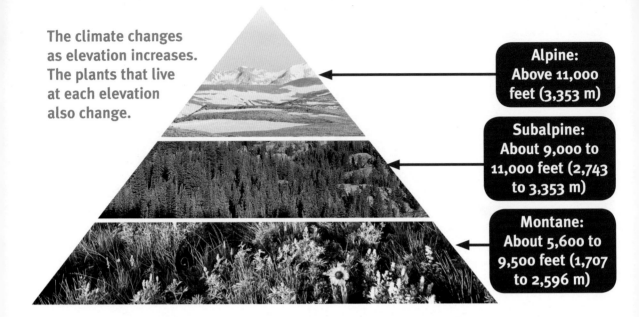

The climate changes as elevation increases. The plants that live at each elevation also change.

Alpine: Above 11,000 feet (3,353 m)

Subalpine: About 9,000 to 11,000 feet (2,743 to 3,353 m)

Montane: About 5,600 to 9,500 feet (1,707 to 2,596 m)

Montane

In the park's lowest elevations, visitors explore montane forests and meadows. These regions are dry and rocky, with warm summers and mild winters. Giant ponderosa pines, the park's tallest trees, are common. So are other evergreens including lodgepole pines and Douglas firs. These trees don't grow very densely. Meadows are wide-open spaces with a variety of grasses and wildflowers. Low shrubs such as juniper and cinquefoil grow in meadows, too.

Subalpine Forest

Above about 9,000 feet (2,743 m), the climate cools and becomes wetter. This subalpine forest supports pines, spruces, and firs that grow closer together than in montane areas. In spring, pale wildflowers such as arnica and columbine blanket the ground. In the region's upper limits, winds are incredibly strong. "Flag trees" have branches on only one side, where winds don't tear them off. Winds damage any twigs or branches that grow against the winds' direction.

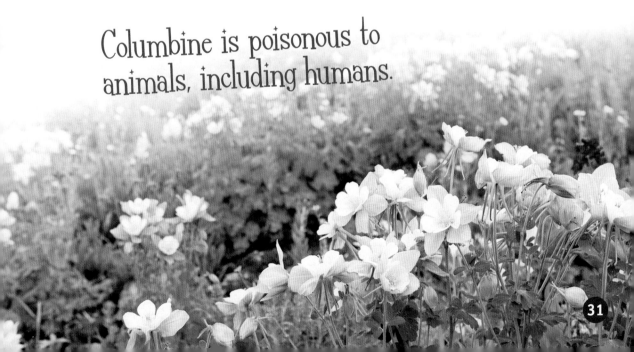

Columbine is poisonous to animals, including humans.

Alpine Tundra

Above 11,000 feet (3,353 m), at the tree line or **timberline**, trees can no longer grow. Here lies the **tundra**. The sun beats down, and winds reach up to 100 miles (161 km) per hour. Temperatures stay low, and little rain falls. Only short plants, able to escape the wind and keep close to the warm soil, live here. Their stems and leaves may have a waxy coating or tiny hairs. These protect them from the sun's harsh rays and keep in heat and moisture.

Elk graze on the short plants that grow in the tundra.

The old-man-of-the-mountain, or alpine sunflower, may take 70 years to bloom.

Despite the harsh environment, the tundra is filled with beauty. Short grasses, mosses, and herbs are abundant. Wildflowers of red, purple, white, and yellow carpet the landscape. Some of these flowers spend their entire lifetimes preparing to bloom. The old-man-of-the-mountain is a sunflower that spends years collecting energy in its roots. When it has stored enough, its bright yellow flowers bloom—but only once. Then the plant dies.

CHAPTER 5

Trouble in the Park

Rocky Mountain National Park is among the most beautiful places in the United States. Rangers work hard every day to protect what makes it special. Sometimes this is a difficult task. The millions of people who visit every year create stress on the environment they are coming to enjoy. Some issues have long-reaching, possibly permanent effects.

Rocky has almost 200 permanent employees and more than 2,000 volunteers.

People Problems

The park's plants and animals suffer because of humans. Visitors trample plants, bother animals, and wear down trails. Bears and other wildlife can begin to rely on human food, breaking into tents, cars, or coolers where they smell it. In addition, cars sometimes hit animals trying to cross roadways. Some animals even lose their natural fear of humans. No longer scared to get close, they may threaten or even attack people. These animals must sometimes be destroyed.

Over time, visitors contribute to wear and tear in one of the nation's most popular parks.

A Day in the Life of a Ranger

The National Park Service employs rangers in parks all over the country. Rangers are officers who protect the park and its visitors. Rangers spend a lot of their time outside. They see if trails need upkeep. They make sure visitors follow the rules designed to keep them safe and to protect the land and animals. They track the weather and other potential hazards and post warnings. Rangers also act as educators, talking with tour groups or visiting schools. And if a visitor is sick, lost, or injured, rangers are often the first responders who come to the rescue.

City lights can affect the night sky in areas that are miles away.

Too Much to Handle

Some threats from human activity, such as air pollution and light pollution, are larger than the individuals who visit Rocky. Global climate change is one of these. As Earth gradually becomes warmer, plants and animals in the mountains slowly move higher to where temperatures are cooler. But there is only so far they can go. Eventually, they will be unable to find a climate in which they can survive. As a result, large numbers of species may someday die out at an alarming rate.

People can help, though. If you visit Rocky or another park, follow the rules and take care to leave no trace of your visit. Help fight climate change by fighting air pollution. Try using less electricity. Look for "climate friendly" energy sources such as solar power. Bike or walk instead of driving whenever possible. You can also try sharing rides with friends. With some thought and effort, we can all help care for the environment. Rocky and all our national parks will benefit. ★

We have to work together to make sure many future generations can enjoy Rocky Mountain National Park.

Map Mystery

What is Rocky Mountain National Park's highest lake? Follow the directions below to find the answer.

Directions

1. Start at the Kawuneeche Visitor Center on the western side of the park.

2. Travel north to La Poudre Pass, where you can check out the source of the Colorado River.

3. Head east to Bridal Veil Falls.

4. You're almost there! Head south and slightly west to Longs Peak, the park's tallest mountain.

5. Finally, hike west to find a high and chilly lake—and solve the mystery!

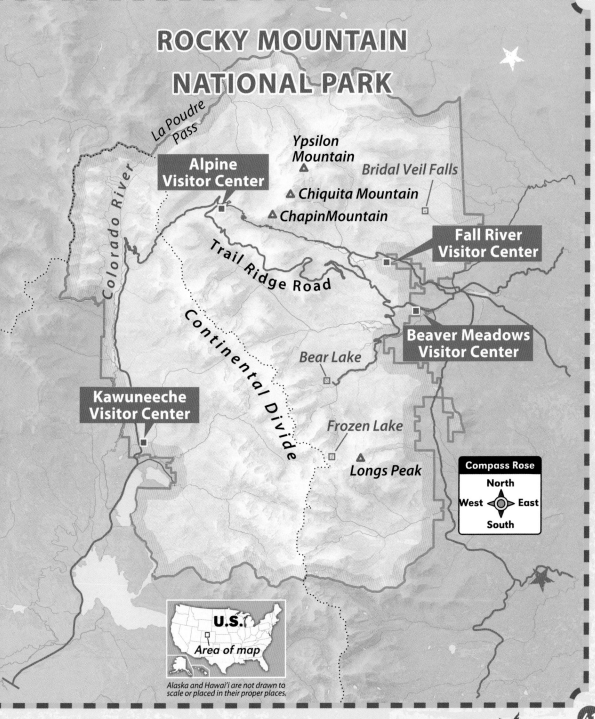

ROCKY MOUNTAIN NATIONAL PARK

La Poudre Pass

Colorado River

Alpine Visitor Center

Ypsilon Mountain ▲

Bridal Veil Falls

▲ Chiquita Mountain

▲ ChapinMountain

Fall River Visitor Center

Trail Ridge Road

Continental Divide

Beaver Meadows Visitor Center

Bear Lake

Kawuneeche Visitor Center

Frozen Lake

▲ Longs Peak

Compass Rose

North

West ◆ East

South

U.S.

Area of map

Alaska and Hawai'i are not drawn to scale or placed in their proper places.

Answer: Frozen Lake

Be an Animal Tracker!

If you're ever in Rocky Mountain National Park, keep an eye out for these animal tracks. They'll help you know which animals are in the area.

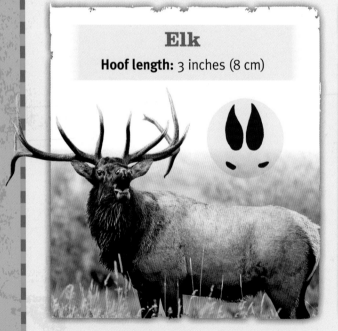

Elk
Hoof length: 3 inches (8 cm)

Moose
Hoof length: 6 inches (16 cm)

Black Bear
Paw length: 4.5 inches (11 cm)

Coyote
Paw length: 2.5 inches (6 cm)

Beaver
Front paw length: 3 inches (8 cm)

Wild Turkey
Foot length: 4.5 inches (11 cm)

True Statistics

Average number of people who visit Rocky Mountain National Park each year: 3.1 million

Combined length of all the park's trails: About 350 miles (563 km)

Height of Longs Peak, the park's tallest mountain: 14,259 feet (4,346 m)

Number of mountain peaks above 12,000 feet (3,658 m): More than 60

Number of mountain peaks above 14,000 feet (4,267 m): 1

Number of lakes: 147

Number of mammal species living in the park: About 60

Number of bird species in the park: About 270

Number of amphibian species in the park: 4

Number of reptile species in the park: 2

Did you find the truth?

T Rocky Mountain National Park has trees that have branches on only one side.

F The park is home to a large population of gray wolves.

Resources

Books

Benoit, Peter. *Tundra*. New York: Children's Press, 2011.

Gregory, Josh. *Moose*. New York: Children's Press, 2016.

Somervill, Barbara A. *Colorado*. New York: Children's Press, 2014.

Visit this Scholastic website for more information on Rocky Mountain National Park:
★ www.factsfornow.scholastic.com
Enter the keywords **Rocky Mountain National Park**

Important Words

climate (KLYE-mit) the weather typical of a place over a long period of time

ecosystems (EE-koh-sis-tuhmz) all the living things in a place and their relation to their environment

elevations (el-uh-VAY-shuhnz) heights above sea level

endangered (en-DAYN-jurd) in danger of becoming extinct, usually because of human activity

erosion (i-ROH-zhuhn) the wearing away of something by water or wind

hypothermia (hye-poh-THUR-mee-uh) the condition of having a dangerously low body temperature

migrating (MYE-grate-ing) moving to another area or climate at a particular time of year

montane (mahn-TAYN) having to do with mountains

species (SPEE-sheez) one of the groups into which animals and plants of the same genus are divided; members of the same species can mate and have offspring

timberline (TIM-bur-line) the highest point at which trees can grow on a mountain, or, in the arctic regions, the farthest northern point where trees can grow

tundra (TUHN-druh) a very cold area where there are no trees and the soil under the surface of the ground is always frozen

Index

Page numbers in **bold** indicate illustrations.

About the Author

Jennifer Zeiger lives in Chicago, Illinois, where she writes and edits books for children.